How to Talk BA

Critical Terminology for Anyone Involved with Business Analysis

Elizabeth Larson, CBAP, PMI-PBA, PMP & Richard Larson, CBAP, PMI-PB/

Watermark Learning

Watermark Learning Publications | Minneapolis, Minnesota

Books published by Watermark Publications are available at special discounts for volume purchases by corporations, institutions, and other organizations. For more information, please email us at Products@WatermarkLearning.com, or call +1-952-921-0900 x204. Volume purchase information and one-time or ongoing licensing details are available online at www.WatermarkLearning.com/products/bundles.php and www.WatermarkLearning.com/courseware-licensing.php.

Portions copyrighted by International Institute of Business Analysis (IIBA®). Portions of materials used with permission from Project Management Institute (PMI).

Disclaimer: Page and section references to the Business Analysis Body of Knowledge (BABOK®) are accurate at time of this publication. Page and section numbers are subject to change without notice by the IIBA®. This Guide may contain typographical or other errors. We strive to eliminate them all. Please see the sections marked "Feedback" and "Updates" in this guide, for information related to providing feedback.

ISBN: 978-0-692-73165-9
Version 1.0

Cover Design
AdVanced Design, Inc.
www.advanceddesign-online.com

Watermark Learning Publications
5001 American Blvd. W.,, Suite 900
Minneapolis, MN, 55437 USA
Telephone: +1 952-921-0900

To project professionals everywhere who are committed to improving their business analysis skills and knowledge

Purpose
Description
Strengths
Limitations

Contents

Our Story

Since 1992, Watermark Learning has been cultivating today's problem solvers and tomorrow's leaders through Business Analysis, Project Management, Agile, and Business Relationship Management training and coaching, and certification preparation. Our clients receive skill development enabling organizations and individuals to define, analyze, and deliver products and services that produce bottom-line results.

We maximize productivity because our focused training and coaching are engaging and immediately applicable. Our certification products and services expertly prepare candidates to pass their exam. Experience our unique combination of best practices, practical approach, and engaging delivery, and you will discover why organizations prefer the Watermark Learning portfolio of services.

Live Training: Our instructor-led courses cover today's most relevant topics to help you keep pace in today's demanding business environment. Attend classes in a traditional classroom setting or through virtual delivery using the Internet.

Private Training and Coaching: Minimize scheduling hassles and travel expenses by inviting a Watermark Learning expert to your site. Your project teams will benefit from lower per-student cost and personalized learning that addressees your organization's particular methods, corporate culture, and business problems.

Public Classes: When you need to train one person or a few people, our open-enrollment classes provide you flexibility. We offer several iterations of core classes throughout the year. You can "sample" our training before committing to an on-site class. In-person and virtual options are available.

Courseware Licensing: Jump-start your own training programs by licensing our high-quality course materials. Teach classes with your own instructors, customize them to your needs, or contract with us for a turnkey solution.

Anytime Learning: Anytime Learning is a great way to take courses you cannot attend in person or virtually, including courses to prepare you for certification exams. You receive the same class materials and instructors as our virtual classes, plus the ability to contact the instructor via email and to proceed at your own pace.

Certification Programs: If you want a skill-based Business Analysis, Project Management, or Agile program, obtain a Masters Certificate from Auburn University and expand your career horizons. If you desire an industry certification, we offer best-in-class PMP®, PMI-PBA®, PMI-ACP®, CBAP®/CCBA®/ECBA®, BRMP®, and CSM®/CSPO® programs.

"Course materials were clear and concise and the exercises were excellent—make sense in my real world. Instructor was also very, very good—shared knowledge and experiences with us without making that the central point. Every minute was valuable. Thanks!"

Michelle Webb, Allianz Life Insurance

_____

Watermark

Introduction

Thank you for choosing Watermark Learning's *How to Speak BA Reference Summary*. The primary purpose of this volume is to help students and practitioners grasp or refresh their understanding of the main terminology in business analysis, including the *Business Analysis Body of Knowledge* (*BABOK® Guide*) and *Business Analysis for Practitioners: A Practice Guide*.

This reference is perfect for anyone who wants a high-level overview of common business analysis concepts and terms, whether you are new to the industry or have been practicing for years and want to keep current. It is also indispensable for anyone studying for the CBAP/CCBA certification or the ECBA certificate to grasp the terms used on the those exams. It also serves as a reference for those who practice business analysis using the *BABOK® Guide* as a standard. It will also prove valuable for anyone in need of a reference guide to definitions of technical business terms used primarily in business analysis.

BABOK Terminology Reference Summary

BA Term	Definition/Use	Reference (BABOK® Guide section unless noted)[1]	Synonyms/Notes
Activities, Business Analysis	A list of activities needed to produce deliverables during a change.	3.1.4.3	Tasks.
Acceptance and Evaluation Criteria Definition	Technique for determining factors that can be used as criteria for evaluating and accepting a design or solution. • **Acceptance criteria** are the minimum requirements to be met for a solution to be worth implementing. • **Evaluation criteria** are measures that will be used to choose between multiple solutions.	10.1.2	
Activity Diagram	UML (Unified Modeling Language) equivalent of a process model. Activity diagrams show the sequential work flow, the decisions made, inputs and outputs, and optionally the organization units involved.	10.35.3 Figure 10.35.3	Process Map/ Workflow Diagram.

1   We have included a list of references with full attributions at the end of this book. The names used in this column are shortened for convenience.

BA Term	Definition/Use	Reference (BABOK® Guide section unless noted)[1]	Synonyms/Notes
Actor	The person or system external to the solution who interacts with the solution as modeled in a use case.	10.47, Glossary	Primary Actor. See Secondary Actor.
Affinity Map	A collaborative technique that helps draw out common themes when a large amount of information is available, but unorganized. It helps to organize product features or themes and can reveal possible root causes of problems or possible solutions.	10.10.3.4	Affinity Diagram.
Agile	An adaptive approach to creating products such as software. It is based on the Agile Manifesto, whose purpose is "uncovering better ways of developing software and helping others do it." Under Agile, business analysis work is performed "just in time" as needed rather than in one phase ahead of time.	Agile Manifesto Watermark Agile Business Analysis	See Scrum.
Allocation	Assigning of requirements to solution components, such as releases. Traces a requirement through design, development, testing, and implementation. Ensures that the completed solution conforms to approved requirements.	7.5.4.3, Glossary	Requirements Allocation.
Alternate Path or Scenario	Any scenario that deviates from the primary path, whether they are variations, errors, or exceptions. They may reconnect with the primary path or have their own ending to the use case.	10.47.3.2	Alternative Flow.

BA Term	Definition/Use	Reference (BABOK® Guide section unless noted)[1]	Synonyms/Notes
Analogous Estimation	The *BABOK Guide* says it is examining components in a work breakdown structure. This definition differs from what is commonly thought to be analogous estimating.	10.19.3.1	
	A top-down approach that uses past projects to estimate a current effort. It uses historical data to help estimate a new effort. For example, a past effort of equivalent scope took 3 months; the new project will take roughly 3 months. Factors for differences in projects can be taken into account. For example, based on historical data the new application previous similar efforts took about 5,000 hours. However, due to technical complexity, we will add an additional 25%.	Larson & Larson, p. 123	See Estimate.
Approach	Established ways to perform business analysis work, including the timing, sequencing, deliverables, and techniques used. Common approaches mentioned in the *BABOK Guide* include: **Predictive** and **Adaptive**.	3.1.8	Methodology, Framework. See Business Analysis Approach.
Association	In UML (Unified Modeling Language), these are relationships between things, such as actors and use cases. Other common uses are for relationships between classes in a data model.	10.47.3.1	Relationship, Interface.

BA Term	Definition/Use	Reference (BABOK® Guide section unless noted)[1]	Synonyms/Notes
Associative Entity	An entity that resolves a many-to-many relationship in a data model. Functioning as "cross-reference" files, associative entities provide flexibility in data. Example: "A Product can be obtained from one or more Suppliers and a Supplier can supply one or more Products." The associative entity might be called "Product Supplier" and it permits any number of suppliers for a product.	Simsion, p. 93, Watermark Data Modeling	Intersection Entity, Resolution Entity. See Many-to-Many.
Actor	The person or system external to the solution who interacts with the solution as modeled in a use case.	10.47, Glossary	Primary Actor. See Secondary Actor.
Approve Requirements	The process of obtaining agreement on and approval of requirements and designs.	5.5	
Assumption	Factors that are considered to be true and that haven't been proven so. The *BABOK Guide* mentions that strategy, scope, and requirements are affected by assumptions, constraints, and dependencies.	6.2.4.10, 10.7.3.3, Glossary	
Attribute (Data)	In data modeling, the individual facts about an entity or class. Attributes in an entity have specific data types and usually have constraints on the values they can accept.	10.15.3.2	Fields in a file or columns in a table.

BA Term	Definition/Use	Reference (BABOK® Guide section unless noted)[1]	Synonyms/Notes
Attributes, Common Requirements	• **Absolute reference**—unique identifier. Not to be altered or reused if the requirement is moved, changed or deleted. • **Author** of the requirement. If the requirement is ambiguous the author may be consulted for clarification. • **Complexity**—how hard a requirement will be to implement. • **Ownership**—individual or group needing the requirement or who will be the business owner after the product is released. • **Priority**—the relative importance of the requirement or the implementation sequence. • **Risks**—uncertain events that may impact requirements. • **Source** of the requirement. All requirements need a source with authority to specify and approve them. • **Stability**—how mature the requirement is. Used to determine if a requirement is firm enough to start work on. • **Status** of the requirement currently, indicating whether it is proposed, accepted, verified with the users, or implemented. • **Urgency**—when requirement is needed. Specify separately from Priority only when implementation deadline exists.	3.4.4.6	

BA Term	Definition/Use	Reference (BABOK® Guide section unless noted)[1]	Synonyms/Notes
Backlog			See Product Backlog.
Baseline	A point established as a reference or checkpoint against which requirements or other changes are compared. Each time requirements are approved they are baselined, which means that the approved version of the requirements is recognized as the official version. Changes to requirements requested after being baselined are handled by a change control process.	Larson and Larson, Glossary	See Change Control.
	(Specific to requirements)) A snapshot in time that represents the current agreed-upon, reviewed, and approved set of requirements, often defining the contents of a specific product release or development iteration. Serves as a basis for further development work.	Wiegers and Beatty, Glossary	
	An approved version of a work product (requirements, scope, etc.) that is used as a basis for comparison and that requires a change control process to change.	*Business Analysis for Practitioners: A Practice Guide* (referred to as BA Practice Guide, Glossary)	

BA Term	Definition/Use	Reference (BABOK® Guide section unless noted)[1]	Synonyms/Notes
Benchmarking	Technique for comparing an organization with its peers and competitors to assess relative strengths and weaknesses.	10.4.1	Market Analysis. See Competitive Analysis.
	Used to compare such things as practices and processes, in other organizations in order to improve and measure performance.	BA Practice Guide, Glossary[2]	
Bottom-Up Estimation	By estimating detailed individual tasks and activities, they can be "rolled up" into an overall estimate. Said to be the most accurate. Example: get estimates for each BA task for a project, then compile into a total estimate.	10.19.3.1	See Estimate.
	The resources doing the work provide activities and estimates to the project manager, who rolls them up often by deliverable, giving an approximation of the effort to complete each business analysis deliverable. Tends to be used with a predictive life cycle, but can be useful when estimating the tasks in the sprint plan on an Agile/Scrum project.	Larson & Larson, p. 124.	
BPMN	Business Process Model and Notation. A visual business process modeling standards that is often used with process design and automated process modeling software.	10.35.3	

2   Project Management Institute. *Business Analysis for Practitioners: A Practice Guide*. Newtown Square, PA: Project Management Institute, Inc., 2015. Copyright and all rights reserved. Material from this publication has been reproduced with the permission of PMI.

BA Term	Definition/Use	Reference (BABOK® Guide section unless noted)[1]	Synonyms/Notes
Brainstorming	A technique that promotes divergent thinking, to produce a broad or diverse set of options. It works best by focusing on one problem or issue.	10.5.1	
Budgeting	A requirements prioritization technique that chooses work based on a budget or a fixed deadline, including regular software package upgrades. Requirements are prioritized based on what can be accomplished with the available resources.	10.33.3.3	Time-Boxing.
Business Analysis	"The practice of enabling **change** in an enterprise by defining **needs** and recommending **solutions** that deliver **value** to **stakeholders**."	1.2, 2.2, Glossary	
	Completing a set of activities to identify needs (problems and opportunities) and recommend solutions to address the need. Business analysis encompasses eliciting, documenting, and managing requirements.	BA Practice Guide Glossary[3]	

3   Project Management Institute. *Business Analysis for Practitioners: A Practice Guide.* Newtown Square, PA: Project Management Institute, Inc., 2015. Copyright and all rights reserved. Material from this publication has been reproduced with the permission of PMI.

BA Term	Definition/Use	Reference (BABOK® Guide section unless noted)[1]	Synonyms/Notes
Business Analysis Approach	"Business analysis approaches describe the overall method that will be followed when performing business analysis work on a given initiative, how and when tasks will be performed, and the deliverables that will be produced."	3.1.2, 3.5.3, Glossary	See Approach.
Business Analysis Plan	The planned activities the Business Analyst will execute to perform the business analysis work. Note that the *BABOK Guide* emphasizes "approach" over a "plan."	3.1.8, Glossary	See Requirements Management Plan.
Business Analysis Information	Represents the inputs, outputs, and work products of business analysis. It can be from the lowest level of detail to the highest. Examples of business analysis information include: needs, requirements, designs, goals, elicitation results, issues, risks, and solution performance measures.	2.2, 3.1.4.2, Glossary	
Business Analysis Planning and Monitoring	The tasks and outputs for planning and organizing business analysis activities with stakeholders and for monitoring business analysis work to ensure it produces desired outcomes. The outputs produced are used as guidelines to other tasks (vs. as direct inputs) in the *BABOK Guide*.	1.4.2, Chapter 3	

BA Term	Definition/Use	Reference (BABOK® Guide section unless noted)[1]	Synonyms/Notes
Business Analyst	"A business analyst is any person who performs business analysis activities, no matter what their job title or organizational role. Business analysts are responsible for discovering, synthesizing, and analyzing information from a variety of sources within an enterprise, including tools, processes, documentation, and stakeholders." The business analyst is responsible for eliciting the actual needs of stakeholders.	1.3, 2.4.1, Glossary	Systems Analyst, Business Systems Analyst See Business Analysis.
	Role whose primary function is to work with stakeholders and elicit, specify, validate, and manage requirements.	Wiegers and Beatty, Glossary	
Business Architecture	Models the enterprise by grouping business operations, functional accountability, business activity, and economic activity, whether in a current or future state. Its purpose is to align strategy and execution around the important activities of a business and to create a framework for planning and managing.	6.1.4.6, 11.4, Glossary	See Enterprise Architecture.
Business Capability Analysis	A specialized technique that describes what an enterprise is able to do. Generates a shared understanding of purpose, risk, priorities, and outcomes.	10.6	See Capability.

BA Term	Definition/Use	Reference (BABOK® Guide section unless noted)[1]	Synonyms/Notes
Business Case	Facilitates decision-making by providing information useful for evaluating whether to fund projects to solve problems or seize opportunities. They provide justification and the rationale for projects based on benefits provided vs. costs and risks of generating them.	10.7.2, Glossary	
Business Goal	Describes a broad target or state that a business aims for to support its strategy and vision. The *BABOK Guide* mentions these are usually expressed qualitatively such as "improve customer satisfaction levels with the ordering process."	6.2.4.1, Glossary	See Goal and Business Objective
Business Need	Description of a problem or opportunity of strategic or tactical importance. They are often triggered by an issue in the organization such as revenue decline or discovery of cost overruns. They may be identified **top-down**, **bottom-up**, **middle management**, or from **external drivers**.	1.4.2, 6.1.4.1, Glossary	Problem, Opportunity. See Need.
Business Objective	Describes a specific state or condition the business strives for to support its goals and vision. Usually expressed with measures and a time frame, e.g., "reduce customer complaints on late deliveries over the next year by 20%."	6.2.4.1, Glossary	Specific, Measurable, Achievable, Relevant, Time-bounded. See Business Goal.

BA Term	Definition/Use	Reference (BABOK® Guide section unless noted)[1]	Synonyms/Notes
Business Requirements	"A representation of goals, objectives and outcomes that describe why a change has been initiated and how success will be assessed. They can apply to the whole of an enterprise, a business area, or a specific initiative."	2.3, Glossary	Business Goals and Objectives.
	Describe the higher-level needs of the organization, such as business issues or opportunities, and provide the rationale for undertaking a project.	BA Practice Guide, Glossary[4]	
Business Rule	A business rule describes a policy, guideline, standard, or regulation upon which the business operates. A Business Rule is a statement that defines or constrains some aspect of the business, and transcends any given project. A specific, practicable, and testable directive.	10.9.2, Glossary	Business Policy.

---

4   Project Management Institute. *Business Analysis for Practitioners: A Practice Guide*. Newtown Square, PA: Project Management Institute, Inc., 2015. Copyright and all rights reserved. Material from this publication has been reproduced with the permission of PMI.

BA Term	Definition/Use	Reference (BABOK® Guide section unless noted)[1]	Synonyms/Notes
	"Business rules describe decisions in the form of self-imposed business constraints. A business rule limits how the organization is run and transcends projects." Examples of business rules can include such things as calculations/computations, sequence (one thing must be performed before something else), limits (number of times something can happen), frequency of events, policies, standard business practices, and data relationship rules of cardinality and optionality).	Larson and Larson, Glossary, pp. 63–64	
	Business constraints that are enforced by data and/or processes	BA Practice Guide, Glossary[5]	
Business Rules Analysis	A specialized technique for identifying and assessing business rules that shape business behavior and guide decision making.	10.9	

5   Project Management Institute. *Business Analysis for Practitioners: A Practice Guide*. Newtown Square, PA: Project Management Institute, Inc., 2015. Copyright and all rights reserved. Material from this publication has been reproduced with the permission of PMI.

BA Term	Definition/Use	Reference (BABOK® Guide section unless noted)[1]	Synonyms/Notes
Capability	The capacity for accomplishing goals or objectives, including activities, knowledge, products and services, functions supported, and decision-making methods. The *BABOK Guide* addresses capabilities in the context of a capability-centric enterprise view to find new uses for existing capabilities.	6.1.4.3, 10.6.3.1, Glossary	See Business Capability Analysis. See Organizational Capability.
Cardinality	The degree of a relationship between two entities, usually represented as "one" or "many."	Simsion, P. 86	See Entity, Relationship.
Change	A BABOK Core Concept, the term refers to what the *BABOK Guide* says is a "transformation in response to a [business] need," which is similar to describing a project. The implication is that a change may or may not be a project and that business analysis tasks control the change. This kind of change includes and improvement aspect, meaning it is purposeful and intended to add value.	Table 2.1.1	Project, Improvement.
Change Control	The planned process for controlling changes to requirements and designs, including how changes are requested, assessed, and prioritized.	3.3.4.2 Glossary	Change Control Process.

BA Term	Definition/Use	Reference (BABOK® Guide section unless noted)[1]	Synonyms/Notes
Change Management	"Planned activities, tools, and techniques to address the human side of change during a change initiative, primarily addressing the needs of the people who will be most affected by the change."	3.3.4.2, 8.5.4.2, Glossary	Organizational Change Management. Change Control.
Change Strategy, Define	Task definition: "Describes the nature of the change." Some considerations include other possible change strategies, recommendation on the best approach and why it's the best option, value that will be delivered, key stakeholders involved, and some transition strategies needed to get from the current to the future state.	6.4.2, Glossary	Change Strategy.
Class	A UML (Unified Modeling Language) method of depicting an entity in a solution, including its attributes, operations, and relationships. A class represents a distinct concept within the enterprise, and may be a physical item or a logical collection of information.	10.15.3.1	See Entity.
Class Model	Class Models are diagrams showing a set of related classes that exist within the enterprise and the associations that each class has with other classes.	10.15.3.4	Class Diagram. See Entity Relationship Diagram.

BA Term	Definition/Use	Reference (BABOK® Guide section unless noted)[1]	Synonyms/Notes
Communicate Business Analysis Information	Communicating appropriate information to stakeholders at the appropriate time and in the appropriate format.	4.4.2	Communicate Requirements. See Business Analysis Information.
Communication Plan, Business Analysis	A plan for what, to whom, when, and how to communicate on a project. It sets the expectations for communications about business analysis among stakeholders.	Glossary	Project Communication Plan.
Competencies, Underlying	The Knowledge Area that covers fundamental competency information not found in the *BABOK Guide* that BAs are expected to know. Includes **Analytical Thinking and Problem Solving, Behavioral Characteristics, Business Knowledge, Communication Skills, Interaction Skills,** and **Tools & Technology.** The behaviors, characteristics, knowledge, and personal qualities a BA is expected to exhibit.	1.4.4, Section 9	
Competitive Analysis	Structured process that assesses strengths and weaknesses of current and future competitors based on key characteristics of an industry. It supports SWOT analysis by helping to identify opportunities and threats.	Glossary	Competitor Analysis. See SWOT Analysis, Benchmarking.

BA Term	Definition/Use	Reference (BABOK® Guide section unless noted)[1]	Synonyms/Notes
Composite Elements	Group of related primitive or detailed data elements recorded in a Data Dictionary.	10.12.3.3	Composite Data, Group Data.
Concept	Describes business objects with a descriptive rather than a data-centric name. It uses nouns to describe the concepts and verbs to describe relationships between concepts.	10.11.3	See Entity, Class.
Concept Model	Identifies a group of "correct" terms used by stakeholders to identify their primary objects such as customer, policy, and claim. It clarifies terms to use in communications, including all business analysis information.	10.11.2	
Configuration Management	Managing changes to the features and functions of a product throughout its life, including documenting them.	3.3.4.2, 9.6.2.2	Change Management.
Constraint	An imposition on a project that limits choices a project team can make. Typical categories include: **Business**—time, cost, resources, etc.; **Technical**—software, databases, hardware, etc.; **External**—regulatory, industry, etc.	6.2.4.3, Glossary	

BA Term	Definition/Use	Reference (BABOK® Guide section unless noted)[1]	Synonyms/Notes
Context	A BABOK Core Concepts, the context describes all the relevant environmental factors that surround, influence, and are affected by a change. Changes are never done in a vacuum, but are always performed within a context. The *BABOK Guide* lists many examples of contexts, which fall into three main groups: **Perceptions**: attitudes, behaviors, beliefs; **External**: competitors, culture, governments, seasons, weather; **Internal**: demographics, goals, infrastructure, languages, losses, processes, products, projects, sales, terminology, and technology.	Table 2.1.1, Glossary	Environment.
Context Diagram	A visual depiction of a solution's scope, showing a system, external agents (people, other systems, or events) who interact with it, and high-level data flowing into and out of the system.	10.13.2	Level 0 DFD, Use Case Diagram. See Interface Analysis.
Corrective Action	A change taken to address a problem indicated through performance or other measures.	3.5.2, 3.5.4.4, 10.40.2, 10.40.2.4	
COTS Package	Commercial Off-the-Shelf Package.	Glossary	Software Package.

BA Term	Definition/Use	Reference (BABOK® Guide section unless noted)[1]	Synonyms/Notes
Cost Analysis	A technique in the BPM Perspective that measures the cost of activities, resources, and related items. Attempts to determine the total cost of ownership of a product or service.	11.5.2	Activity Based Costing.
Crow's Foot	A common data modeling notation that designates a "many" side of a relationship. In any relationship that has a "many" in it, a crow's foot represents the "many" side as shown on the right of the example diagram.	Simsion, p. 70, Watermark Data Modeling	See Many-to-Many, One-to-Many.
CRUD Matrix	Create, Read, Update, and Delete matrices. Associates user access rights to data. It can also be used to cross-reference data to process to ensure completeness and relevance.	Glossary	Interaction Diagram.
Customer	*BABOK Guide* Stakeholder definition: "A customer uses or may use products or services produced by the enterprise and may have contractual or moral rights that the enterprise is obliged to meet."	2.4.2, Glossary	
Data Dictionary	Defines the data used or needed by an organization, including primitive and more complex data definitions. It will usually be elaborated into more detailed models such as a Class Model or Entity Relationship Diagram.	10.12.2	

BA Term	Definition/Use	Reference (BABOK® Guide section unless noted)[1]	Synonyms/Notes
Data Extraction Tool	"Data extraction tools allow a user to select a data basket full of variables and then recode those variables into a form that the user desires. The user can then develop customized displays of any selected data."	Data.gov	
Data Flow Diagram	A technique that shows the context of the data that flows into processes, out of them, and is stored by the system.	10.13.2	DFDs.
Data Modeling	A technique for depicting the data requirements for a solution using entities/classes, the relationships or associations between them, and the attributes they contain.	10.15.2	Entity-Relationship Diagrams, Class Diagrams.
Data Model	Provides the information that appears on each interface (screen) for both entry and display. Data models such as an entity/relationship diagram (ERD) contain entities, attributes, and data and business rules, such as whether or not customers are required to have accounts.	Larson & Larson, p. 56	
Decision Analysis	A technique that explores the important aspects of a decision amidst uncertainty and/or a limited number of alternatives, such as a choice between alternative solutions.	10.16.2, Glossary	

BA Term	Definition/Use	Reference (BABOK® Guide section unless noted)[1]	Synonyms/Notes
Decomposition	Breaking down something higher-level into simpler subsets for the purpose of studying or analyzing it. This technique is often presented using graphical models.	Glossary	See Functional Decomposition.
Defect	A flaw in a deliverable that either lessens its quality, or causes it to vary from its preferred characteristics. Defective requirements may include: incorrect, incomplete, missing, or conflicting.	Glossary	See Requirements Defect.
Deliverable	A unique output from a process that has been agreed will be delivered, such as documents, diagrams, business rules, or other work products.	1.4.3.8, 3.1.4.2, Glossary	
	A "product, result, or capability" that is both unique and verifiable and that is used to complete a "process, phase, or project."	BA Practice Guide, Glossary[6]	
	"A tangible output from a project, project phase, or process." A few examples of deliverables are planning deliverables (ex. Work Breakdown Structure or budget), business analysis deliverables (ex. results from a requirements workshop, use case model, and a data dictionary), and testing deliverables (ex. results from a user acceptance test, acceptance criteria, or test scenarios).	Larson and Larson, Glossary	Artifact, Work Product.

6   Project Management Institute. *Business Analysis for Practitioners: A Practice Guide*. Newtown Square, PA: Project Management Institute, Inc., 2015. Copyright and all rights reserved. Material from this publication has been reproduced with the permission of PMI.

BA Term	Definition/Use	Reference (BABOK® Guide section unless noted)[1]	Synonyms/Notes
Delphi Estimation	Queries experts privately for opinions in 2 or more rounds, and provides feedback from the other estimates. It involves iterative revisions until a preset number (average is 3) of rounds are complete or until group consensus is reached for the final estimate. Relies on expert judgment and history to be effective. **Example**: Round 1, estimates are 900, 1200, and 2000 hours. Round 2: 1100 to 1800. Round 3: 1400 hours is reached as the consensus.	10.19.3.1	See Estimate.
Denormalization	The process of reducing the normal forms of some entities in a data model to increase database performance. It often results in fewer tables, which reduces database joins.	Simsion, p. 60, Watermark Data Modeling	See Normalization.
Dependency	Identify logical relationships, such as which activities have to be completed before subsequent tasks can begin. Requirements can have dependencies, such as the Depends type of relationship.	5.1.4.2, 6.3.4.2, 10.47.3.1	Depends Relationship.
Derivation	Identifies the "lineage" of a requirement by tracing it back to the business need, or to another requirement.	5.1.4.2	Derive Relationship.

BA Term	Definition/Use	Reference (BABOK® Guide section unless noted)[1]	Synonyms/Notes
Design	"A design is a usable representation of a solution." What this means is that it can be used to translate into a solution that can be built to address a business need. Compare this with requirements, which represent a usable form of a business need.	2.2, Glossary	"To-Be" Requirements.
Document Analysis	A technique that collects requirements for an existing ("As Is") system by studying and summarizing available documentation. It gathers details of a current system in two broad categories: 1) Business documentation, 2) System documentation.	10.18.2, Glossary	
Domain	An area of the enterprise being studied or analyzed, usually for the purpose of addressing a business need. It often corresponds to organizational boundaries, but may be broader and include stakeholders outside of the organization.	Glossary	Problem Domain.
	The domain is the scope or area of interest, whether something managed (project and product scope), worked in (business domain) or problem/opportunity (problem domain).	Larson and Larson, Glossary	

BA Term	Definition/Use	Reference (BABOK® Guide section unless noted)[1]	Synonyms/Notes
Domain Subject Matter Expert	*BABOK Guide* Stakeholder definition: "A domain subject matter expert is any individual with in-depth knowledge of a topic relevant to the business need or solution scope. This role is often filled by people who may be end users or people who have in-depth knowledge of the solution such as managers, process owners, legal staff, consultants, and others."	2.4.3, Glossary	See SME.
Elicit Requirements	Bring out or draw out requirements, through actively engaging stakeholders. It is done throughout a change and the various elicitation techniques are inter-connected. Includes the tasks of **P**repare for Elicitation, **C**onduct Elicitation, **C**onfirm Elicitation Results, **C**ommunicate Business Analysis information, and Manage Stakeholder **C**ollaboration.	Section 4, Figure 4.0.1	Gather, Collect, Capture Requirements. See Elicitation and Collaboration.
Elicitation and Collaboration	This Knowledge Area (KA) is focused on actively engaging stakeholders to obtain information such as requirements. The *BABOK Guide* mentions 3 major types: **Collaborative**, **Research**, and **Experiments**.	1.4.2, Section 4, 4.2.2, Glossary	See Elicit Requirements.
End User	*BABOK Guide* Stakeholder definition: "End users are stakeholders who directly interact with the solution. End users can include all participants in a business process, or who use the product or solution."	2.4.4, Glossary	

BA Term	Definition/Use	Reference (BABOK® Guide section unless noted)[1]	Synonyms/Notes
Enterprise	The *BABOK Guide* uses this term to refer to the parts of one or more organizations that are or could be undergoing a change. For business analysis, the scope of an enterprise corresponds with the scope of the change. Note the formal definition in the *BABOK Guide* mentions an enterprise as "a system of one or more organizations." This definition makes more sense when external stakeholders are included in a change.	2.2, Glossary	
Enterprise Architecture	Describes major current and future domains and the relationships needed to run an organization that integrate into a complete framework. It includes both the organizational (people, processes, operations) and technical (software, hardware, IT) dimensions.	2.2.3, 5.2.3, Glossary	See Business Architecture.
Enterprise Readiness Assessment	An assessment of an enterprise's ability to incorporate a solution or change and to put it to effective use. The goal is to avoid solutions that are not used or used fully.	6.4.4.3, Glossary	Organizational Readiness Assessment.

BA Term	Definition/Use	Reference (BABOK® Guide section unless noted)[1]	Synonyms/Notes
Entity	A business object, representing a person, place, thing, process, or event. Used with Entity-Relationship Diagrams (ERDs).	10.15.3.1	Table. See Class, Concept.
Entity Relationship Diagram	Visual/graphical representation of a data structure including entities, attributes, and relationships between entities.	10.15.3.4, Glossary	Data Model, ERD.
Envisioning (Requirements)	Work done at the beginning of a project to get a high-level, common understanding of the scope	Watermark Agile Business Analysis Agile Modeling Blog	Ideation, Product Planning, Customer Discovery.
Epic	Large user stories that need to be broken down into smaller stories before they are implemented. Epics can remain epics until they become high priority on the product backlog and will be implemented in an upcoming iteration.	Watermark Agile Business Analysis	

BA Term	Definition/Use	Reference (BABOK® Guide section unless noted)[1]	Synonyms/Notes
Estimate	The systematic process of projecting the time and costs of doing work and delivering a product/solution taking into account uncertainties and unknowns. The *BABOK Guide* mentions various types of estimates to be familiar with: • top-down (analogous) • bottom-up • parametric • rough order of magnitude (ROM) • rolling wave • Delphi • PERT (three-point estimates)	10.19.2, 10.19.3, Glossary	Estimation.
Event	An external, internal, or temporal occurrence in the business to which the business responds with a process. Events can initiate, interrupt, or terminate a process, and exist outside the process.	10.35.3, 10.44.3, 10.47.3, Glossary	Trigger.

BA Term	Definition/Use	Reference (BABOK® Guide section unless noted)[1]	Synonyms/Notes
Expert Judgment	Used to determine the business analysis approach as well as in techniques such as Acceptance & Evaluation Criteria, Estimation, and Risk Analysis. Expertise may come from a wide variety of "sources including stakeholders on the initiative, organizational Centers of Excellence, consultants, or associations and industry groups."	3.1.5, 10.19.3.3	
Extend Relationship	In use case modeling, a relationship that extends functionality of a use case at predetermined "extension points." The original use case is not dependent on the extending one.	10.47.3.1	Extends Relationship.
External Interface	Any type of interaction outside a solution, including human interaction on a user interface, software interfaces between systems, or hardware interaction.	Glossary	Interface.
Facilitation	Neutrally and collaboratively guiding a group to a predefined outcome. Effective facilitation typically involves a predefined process and structure.	9.5.1.2, Glossary	

BA Term	Definition/Use	Reference (BABOK® Guide section unless noted)[1]	Synonyms/Notes
Facilitator	Someone who guides an elicitation or similar session. Facilitators have the responsibility to:	Table 10.37.1, 10.50.3.2	
	Establish a professional and objective tone for the meeting.		
	Enforce discipline, structure, ground rules for the meeting.		
	Introduce the goals and agenda for the meeting, and above all keep focused on them.		
	Manage the meeting and keep the team on track.		
	Facilitate a process of decision making and build consensus, but avoid participating in the content of the discussion.		
	Ensure all stakeholders participate and their input is heard.		
	Ask the right questions; analyze the information being provided at the session by the stakeholders, and follow-up with probing questions, if necessary.		
Feasibility Study	An initial study to determine whether a solution is viable to accomplish a desired outcome, whether it is to solve a problem or to seize an opportunity. The BABOK Guide lists technical, organizational, and economic as factors to consider.	10.7.3.3, Glossary	

BA Term	Definition/Use	Reference (BABOK® Guide section unless noted)[1]	Synonyms/Notes
Feature	A grouping of related functionality or services that should align with business goals and objectives and meet stakeholder needs. Features have a cohesive set of associated requirements that provide stakeholder value.	Glossary	Function.
	Description of capabilities, characteristics and functions of a product or solution. Examples of features of a smartphone include the camera, texting, ability to swipe to enter text, and access to the internet.	Larson and Larson, Glossary	
	Logically related functions of a system that provide value to business stakeholders.	Wiegers and Beatty, Glossary	
Fishbone Diagram	A type of diagram used in problem analysis for determining possible root causes of business problems. The problem to be solved is placed as the "head" of the "fish" and possible causes and subcauses are the "bones."	10.40.3.1, Glossary	Cause-and-Effect Diagram, Ishikawa Diagram.
Flow	The direction or path of a process. Flows document the primary and alternate paths of a process, and can split at decision points, and potentially later merge back together.	10.35.2, 10.47.3.2	Path.

BA Term	Definition/Use	Reference (BABOK® Guide section unless noted)[1]	Synonyms/Notes
Flow of Events			See Use Case Flow of Events.
Flowchart	Visual image of the work performed in an organization, including who does it and how they collaborate.	10.35.3.1	Process Model. See Swimlane.
Focus Group	A technique used to gather qualitative input about a problem, opportunity, product, system, etc. It can be useful when many ideas need to be generated quickly, especially concerning attitudes and beliefs about a product.	10.21.2, Glossary	
Force Field Analysis	A visual way of showing opposing forces that support and oppose a change. The forces for each side are grouped together pointing toward the middle. An estimate of the strength of each opposing force can help with change management.	10.16.2, Glossary	Decision Analysis.

BA Term	Definition/Use	Reference (BABOK® Guide section unless noted)[1]	Synonyms/Notes
Foreign Key	An attribute that establishes a relationship between one entity and another. It associates one or more occurrences of an entity with usually one occurrence of another. Foreign keys always 1) appear in the "many" end of a one-to-many relationship and 2) replicate the <u>entire</u> Primary Key of the single-valued entity. For example, if a Product has a 3-attribute primary key on the "one" side of a relationship, then the Product ID foreign key contained in Order Item (the "many" side), will also be made up of the same 3 attributes.	Simsion, p. 59, Watermark Data Modeling	See Primary Key.
Functional Decomposition	Identifies the high-level functions of an organization or proposed solution and then breaks down those processes into subprocesses and activities.	10.22.2	See Decomposition.
Functional Requirement	Describes the behavior and/or information that the solution will possess. They represent capabilities the system will be able to perform.	2.3, Glossary	See Requirements Analysis.
Gap Analysis	A formal comparison between anything expected or desired and the current state. Useful in comparing current and future states during strategy analysis.	6.4.4.2, Glossary	Variance Analysis.

BA Term	Definition/Use	Reference (BABOK® Guide section unless noted)[1]	Synonyms/Notes
Generalization Relationship	In use case modeling, a relationship that resembles a parent–child type. The "parent" use case contains the generalized functionality that applies to all of its "children." Each child use case contains specialized flows and possible exceptions unique to the type. For example, a "Process Transaction" parent might have children of "Accept Deposit," "Make Withdrawal," and "Pay Loan."	Watermark Use Case	Subtype/ Supertype.
Given-When-Then	A format for specifying acceptance criteria that carry the detailed requirements for a user story. Most often used on Agile/Scrum efforts and has the format of: --Given \<an initial condition\> (optional) --When I \<perform an action\> --Then I expect \<this result\>.	10.48.3.2	See Acceptance and Evaluation Criteria Definition.
Goal			See Business Goal.
Governance	Standards and guidelines used to control something, such as business analysis, project selection, quality control, approach, or priorities.	3.3.2, Glossary	Governance Process, Business Analysis Governance.

BA Term	Definition/Use	Reference (BABOK® Guide section unless noted)[1]	Synonyms/Notes
Ground Rules	Rules that establish a code for conduct for a group activity and allow a facilitator to enforce discipline if needed.	9.5.1.3, 10.50.3.3	
Hand-Off	In process modeling, a formal passing of a process flow from one role to another, often done along with inputs or outputs.	10.34.2	
Identify Business Analysis Performance Improvements	The process of assessing business analysis work in order to plan for process improvements.	3.5	
Impact Analysis	Before conducting a change, the best way to determine how the change will affect stakeholders is to study it. An impact analysis attempts to determine how the proposed change will impact a group of stakeholders or a system. Traceability is a useful way of doing impact analysis on requirements changes.	5.4.4.2, 8.4.4.2, Glossary	
Implementation Subject Matter Expert	*BABOK Guide* Stakeholder definition: "A stakeholder who has specialized knowledge regarding the implementation of one or more solution components." Examples include "project librarian, change manager, configuration manager, solution architect, developer, database administrator, information architect, usability analyst, trainer, and organizational change consultant."	2.4.5, Glossary	SME.

BA Term	Definition/Use	Reference (BABOK® Guide section unless noted)[1]	Synonyms/Notes
Include Relationship	In use case modeling, a relationship that provides access from one or more use cases to shared functionality in a separate use case. It may be an incomplete use case, and the use cases that refer to it are dependent on it.	10.47.3.1	Subroutine.
Increment	Finite additions to products or other deliverables based on adding one piece at a time vs. building an entire product. (Think of adding one brick to a wall as an increment.)	11.1.1	Release.
Indicator	A particular quantity used to measure progress toward a goal, output, or task. Good indicators are said to have these qualities: Clear, Relevant, Economical, Adequate, Quantifiable, Trustworthy, and Credible.	10.28.3.1 Glossary	See Metric.
Influence	To be a compelling force on or produce effects on others. Proactively shift thinking, actions, and even emotional states of other people.	3.2.4.1, 9.5.2	Leadership.
Inspection	A formal examination of a deliverable or work product by people qualified to evaluate it. An inspection follows a standard process with specific criteria to help identify and ultimately remove defects.	10.37.3.2, Glossary	See Peer Review, Walk-through.

BA Term	Definition/Use	Reference (BABOK® Guide section unless noted)[1]	Synonyms/Notes
Instance	One unique occurrence or example of an entity	Watermark Data Modeling	Row of a database table.
Interface	A connection between two components, whether people, systems, and/or hardware. The *BABOK Guide* in general refers to interfaces as between components (e.g., system-to-system). "User Interface" refers to a user interacting with a system.	10.32.3.3 Glossary	User Interface.
Interface Analysis	A technique that helps define boundaries of a system by defining the interfaces to users, other systems, or system components that provides functionality, inputs, and outputs.	10.24.2	See Context. Diagram.
Interview	A technique that involves systematic questioning of stakeholders to learn about their needs, root causes of them, and the stakeholders' requirements. Interviews may be formal or informal, structured or unstructured, and by individual or group.	10.25.2, Glossary	
Iteration	One execution of a series of steps that when repeated is intended to successively get closer to an intended goal. For example, in software development, each iteration adds another layer of knowledge or complexity to a deliverable. (Think of refining a picture using successive layers until it is finished.)	11.1, Glossary	Cycle.

BA Term	Definition/Use	Reference (BABOK® Guide section unless noted)[1]	Synonyms/Notes
Knowledge Area	"An area of expertise that includes several specific business analysis tasks."	1.4.2, Glossary	Domain.
Lessons Learned Process	A technique that compiles things that both went well and could be improved on projects or project phases. Includes generating preventive actions and is done to incorporate what is learned to improve future performance.	10.27.2, Glossary	Retrospective.
Life Cycle	Specific stages through which an entity or other object passes in sequence during its lifetime (from creation through removal).	Glossary	
Logical Models	Graphical representations used to represent specific functional requirements, such as data or process.	Larson & Larson, p. 54	See Model.
Many-to-Many	A common relationship in a data model in which one instance of an entity is related to multiple instances of another entity and vice versa. For example, a Product can be obtained from one or more Suppliers and a Supplier can supply one or more Products. Both sides of the relationship have a "crow's foot" to indicate "many."	Simsion, p. 91, Watermark Data Modeling	See Crow's Foot, Relationship.

BA Term	Definition/Use	Reference (BABOK® Guide section unless noted)[1]	Synonyms/Notes
Matrix	Matrices are used for tabular information that cross-references other information. Traceability is best and most commonly expressed in a matrix, as are requirements attributes, data dictionary items, CRUD matrices, business rules, etc. Simple tables of information are another form of matrix. More complex matrices have relationships between columns of the matrix for the same row of information.	7.1.4.1, Glossary	Table.
Maslow's Hierarchy of Needs	Physiological, Safety, Love/Belonging, Esteem, Self-Actualization. A common schema for the stages of motivation for individuals	n/a	
Message	Information sent between objects in a sequence diagram, shown as an arrow between the objects. The sequence diagram shows the stimuli flowing between objects. Messages become stimuli that trigger actions and are called events in UML (Unified Modeling Language). Also used in Interface Analysis to describe component communication.	Figure 10.24.1, 10.42.3.3	See Event, Sequence Diagram.
Metadata	Data about data, such as ranges or other constraints on attribute values, code values, volumes of data instances, etc.	10.15.3.5, Glossary	See Data Modeling.

BA Term	Definition/Use	Reference (BABOK® Guide section unless noted)[1]	Synonyms/Notes
	Metadata also may provide other relevant information, such as the responsible steward, associated laws and regulations, and the access management policy.	Data.gov	
Methodology	A repeatable set of methods, steps, and techniques usually performed in a certain sequence and designed to create an output such as software, processes, or training.	Glossary	See Approach.
	A prescribed way for completing a project, project phase, iteration, etc. It usually includes processes and templates and could include roles and project phase names.	Larson and Larson, Glossary	
Metric	A standard of measurement often associated with a goal or the performance of something. It is usually associated with a single point in time. Metrics are said to be specific points, thresholds, or ranges.	10.28.3.2, Glossary	See Indicator.

BA Term	Definition/Use	Reference (BABOK® Guide section unless noted)[1]	Synonyms/Notes
	Quantifiable measures used for the purposed of evaluating something, like a solution or business.	BA Practice Guide, Glossary[7]	
	A measure used to judge the health and success of a project, product, or set of activities, such as the business analysis work.	Larson and Larson, Glossary	
Metrics and Key Performance Indicators	A technique for measuring progress and performance. **Metrics** are meant to measure business performance, like their name implies. **Key Performance Indicators** measure progress towards strategic goals.	10.28.2	KPI.
Milestone	An important event, such as the completion or handoff of key deliverables or the end of a defined phase. Examples include: requirements approved, roles and responsibilities defined, or software vendor contract sent to Legal.	Larson and Larson, p 24	Goal, Target.

7   Project Management Institute. *Business Analysis for Practitioners: A Practice Guide.* Newtown Square, PA: Project Management Institute, Inc., 2015. Copyright and all rights reserved. Material from this publication has been reproduced with the permission of PMI.

BA Term	Definition/Use	Reference (BABOK® Guide section unless noted)[1]	Synonyms/Notes
Model	A template for representing things that may combine text, matrices, and diagrams. Serves as an abstraction of reality to represent some portion of requirements or designs to improve understanding and communication.	7.1.4.1, Glossary	
Monitoring	Tracking performance of a process or an entire solution, typically using baseline data (if possible), data collection, data analysis, and reporting. It is usually done to see actual vs. expected results and to then use the measures to help improve performance.	Glossary	See Indicator, Metric.
MoSCoW Analysis	A requirements prioritization technique, using an acronym to divide requirements into four categories: Must have, Should have, Could have, and Won't have.	Table 11.1.2	MoSCoW Prioritization.
Need	A core concept, a need is a problem or opportunity that serve as a trigger for stakeholders to take action. The *BABOK Guide* points out they may erode or enhance the value of existing solutions and so may be the cause of further needs. Needs could come from internal or external problems or opportunities.	Table 2.1.1, Glossary	See Business Need.

BA Term	Definition/Use	Reference (BABOK® Guide section unless noted)[1]	Synonyms/Notes
Negotiation	"Broadly speaking, **negotiation** is an interaction of influences. Such interactions, for example, include the process of resolving disputes, agreeing upon courses of action, bargaining for individual or collective advantage, or crafting outcomes to satisfy various interests. Negotiation involves two basic elements: the process and the substance."	9.5.4	[Source: Wikipedia.com].
Nonfunctional Requirements	The qualities of a solution over and above its functional capabilities. They are specific conditions a solution must have to be regarded as effective. Refer to the *BABOK Guide* for a list of 15 common categories of nonfunctional requirements, such as efficiency, reliability, security, scalability, and availability.	10.30.3.1, Glossary	Supplementary Specifications, Quality-of-Service Requirements.
	"Requirements that express qualities that a product is required to have, including interface, environment, and quality attribute properties."	BA Practice Guide[8]	

8   Project Management Institute. *Business Analysis for Practitioners: A Practice Guide.* Newtown Square, PA: Project Management Institute, Inc., 2015. Copyright and all rights reserved. Material from this publication has been reproduced with the permission of PMI.

BA Term	Definition/Use	Reference (BABOK® Guide section unless noted)[1]	Synonyms/Notes
	The qualities of a system. Performance, security, and availability are examples of nonfunctional requirements. For example, a functional website that is slow and not always available probably fails to meet two nonfunctional requirements.	Larson and Larson, Glossary	
	A description of a property that a system must exhibit or a constraint that the system must respect.	Wiegers and Beatty, Glossary	
Normal Form	Principles in data modeling that associate with successively higher levels of meaning to the business. • **1st Normal Form**: Attributes must be dependent on its entity and no other entity (i.e., no repeating attributes). • **2nd Normal Form**: Each attribute must be dependent on the entire Unique Identifier, not just a part of a UID. • **3rd Normal Form**: Each attribute must be dependent on nothing but the Unique Identifier, • **4th Normal Form**: Attributes have been moved to entities in which they're required. • **5th Normal Form**: a recursive many-to-many relationship resolved by creating a structure entity.	Simsion, p. 45, Watermark Data Modeling	See Normalization.

BA Term	Definition/Use	Reference (BABOK® Guide section unless noted)[1]	Synonyms/Notes
Normalization	The process of refining a data model to give it increasing levels of meaning to the business. Each successive level is called a "normal form" and is based on mathematical principles. The goal of normalization is to have each attribute be associated with the correct entity.	Simsion, p. 35 Watermark Data Modeling	See Normal Form.
Objective			See Business Objective.
Observation	A technique used to elicit requirements by watching people in their natural work environment. This technique is useful as an adjunct to other elicitation methods; e.g., to fill in gaps.	10.31.2, Glossary	Job Shadowing.
One-to-One, One-to-Many	Two common types of relationships in a data model. • **One-to-One**: An entity has a relationship to one instance of another entity, and vice versa. • **One-to-Many**: Entity A has a relationship to one instance of entity B, and entity B is related to multiple instances of entity A (shown with a "Crow's foot") .	Simsion, p. 89, Watermark Data Modeling	See Crow's Foot.
OLAP	Online analytical processing (OLAP) is a part of business intelligence that allows interactive analysis of large amounts of data. For example, users get drill down, drill up, and drill sideways to get different insights and perspectives on their data.	11.2.2.4, Glossary	

BA Term	Definition/Use	Reference (BABOK® Guide section unless noted)[1]	Synonyms/Notes
Operational Support	*BABOK Guide* Stakeholder definition: "Operational support is responsible for the day-to-day management and maintenance of a system or product."	2.4.6, Glossary	Operations Analyst, Product Analyst, Help Desk, and Release Manager.
Opportunity	One of the two aspects the *BABOK Guide* lists as a business need. It is the potential for adding something beneficial to the enterprise, usually in the form of a new product, market, or service.	Table 2.1.1, 6.1.4.1	See Need.
Opportunity Cost	The cost of not using funds for alternative investments. It happens when nonvalidated projects or requirements get implemented because alternative solutions could have been invested in.	5.4.4.2, 6.4.4.4	
Optionality	In data modeling, any relationship or attribute that is not mandatory. These are typically problematic since program code must enforce the capturing of data when it is needed or not (vs. mandatory data that a database could enforce).	Simsion, p. 71 Watermark Data Modeling	Optional field/column.
Organization	An independent, organized group of people working toward common goals and purposes. An organization is usually under the control of a board or small number of individuals who oversee its management and operations.	2.2, Glossary	Company, Nonprofit.

BA Term	Definition/Use	Reference (BABOK® Guide section unless noted)[1]	Synonyms/Notes
Organization Modeling	A technique to depict the structure of an organization, its functions, and its people. It shows the "scope" of organization units, the relationships between people of that unit, their roles, and how they interface with other units.	10.32.2, Glossary	
Organizational Capability	Enterprise functions such as processes, technologies, and information.	Glossary	See Capability.
Organizational Process Assets	Anything that can be used by an organization to assist with its processes, such as defining, improving, and performing them. For business analysis it can include: elements of existing business analysis approaches used by the organization, corporate governance standards, and templates.	5.2.8	
Parametric Estimation	Using history to come up with a "calibrated parametric model of the element attributes being estimated."	10.19.3.1,	
	Uses parameters, such as number of use cases, processes, or user stories to help estimate a future effort. For example, each use case takes 5 hours to develop, and 10 must be done, so the estimate is 50 hours for use cases.	Larson & Larson p. 123	See Estimate.

BA Term	Definition/Use	Reference (BABOK® Guide section unless noted)[1]	Synonyms/Notes
Peer Review	A review of one or more work products. Can be formal or informal.	Glossary	Audits. Reviews (Techniques 10.37), See Inspection, Walk-through.
PERT Estimation	An estimation technique that uses 3 estimating values: • Optimistic value = best case scenario • Pessimistic value = worst case scenario • Most likely value = most likely scenario PERT is a weighted average so the most likely estimate is multiplied by 4 while the optimistic and pessimistic values carry the weight of 1. **Calculation:** [Optimistic value + Pessimistic value + (4 times the most likely value)] / 6	10.19.3.1	See Estimate.
Plan	A proposal for achieving a goal. "Plans describe events' . . . dependencies . . . the expected sequence . . . schedule . . . outcomes... resources needed."	2.2, Glossary	Note that the Glossary's definition differs from that of the Key Terms in the Key Concepts chapter. This is from the latter.

BA Term	Definition/Use	Reference (BABOK® Guide section unless noted)[1]	Synonyms/Notes
Planning Poker	A form of Delphi estimation using a fixed number of points or chips. Using multiple rounds of voting, the team estimates the relative size of a user story until it reaches consensus on the story size. Often used as a way to estimate user stories on Agile projects.	Larson & Larson, p. 121	See Delphi Estimation, User Story.
Pool	In process modeling using BPMN (Business Process Modeling Notation), pools are broad boundaries and may group multiple swim lanes. Common pools are processes, external customers, the internal organization, external vendors, etc.	10.35.3.1	See Process Modeling.
Predictive Approach	By creating and following a plan, the predictive approach seeks to minimize uncertainties during a change (think project). Used when requirements are fairly well known, when the risk of a failed implementation is high, and when stakeholder availability is low.	3.1.4.1, Glossary	Waterfall, Waterfall Methodology.
Preventive Action	A proactive change made to prevent a possible problem from occurring.	10.40.2	Preventative Action, Proactive Analysis.
Primary Actor			See Actor.

BA Term	Definition/Use	Reference (BABOK® Guide section unless noted)[1]	Synonyms/Notes
Primary Key	In data modeling, the one attribute or combination of attributes that uniquely identifies an instance of an entity.	Simsion, p. 57 Watermark Data Modeling	Unique Identifier. See Entity, Foreign Key, Instance.
Primitive Data	A detailed data element that is grouped with related elements into a Composite element in a Data Dictionary.	10.12.3	Detailed Data Attribute. See Data Dictionary.
Primary Path or Scenario	Refers to the main or simplest scenario, the one with no exceptions that actors follow to accomplish their goal in a use case or business process model.	Watermark Use Case	Primary Flow. See Use Cases and Scenarios.
Process	A series of steps, performed to accomplish a goal, done in response to a trigger, and which transform inputs to outputs.	10.35, Glossary	Procedure.
Process Model	A set of diagrams and supporting text that supports Process Modeling. They describe the sequence of steps that transform inputs into outputs.	10.35.2, Glossary	See Process Modeling.
	Business process maps graphically depict business activities. They chart the course of a process from its beginning (initial input) to its end (final output). These models provide the basis for interface (screen) navigation.	Larson & Larson, p. 55.	See Business Process Model, Process Map.

BA Term	Definition/Use	Reference (BABOK® Guide section unless noted)[1]	Synonyms/Notes
Process Modeling	A technique for visually documenting work performed in an organization, including who does it and how they collaborate. Process models can be used to discover requirements, inputs/outputs, document the BA approach, and uncover stakeholders.	10.35	Flowcharting, Process Analysis, Workflow Modeling. See Process Model.
Process Owner	Person who has the ultimate responsibility for the performance of a process in realizing its objectives measured by key process indicators, and has the authority and ability to make necessary changes.	11.5.2.1	
Product	An output, work product, or artifact that is produced, that can be measured, and is either an end result itself or a component of the end result.	BA Practice Guide	
	A tangible output from a project, project phase, or process.	Larson and Larson, Glossary	AKA Deliverable, Solution, System.
	"The ultimate deliverable a project is developing."	Wieners and Beatty, Glossary	

BA Term	Definition/Use	Reference (BABOK® Guide section unless noted)[1]	Synonyms/Notes
Product Backlog	Used most often in Agile/Scrum, the product backlog is a list of requirement statements, usually written in the form of user stories. This list can be estimated and prioritized and used to select features to be developed each iteration.	10.33.3.2, Glossary	Sprint Backlog. See User Stories.
Product Box	A collaborative game in which the team looks at a project or product through the eyes of the end customer. Participants sketch a "box" for the product and list major features and benefits as if it was being sold in a retail store.	10.10.3.4	
Product Owner	A business stakeholder or representative "responsible for ensuring that the change (project) being developed addresses the requirements for which it has been mandated." A term adopted by the Scrum framework for the person designated to make product-related decisions during Agile/Scrum projects, especially during sprints. Among other things, product owners also set priorities for features to be worked on during sprints.	11.1.2.2, Larson and Larson, p. 26	See Domain Subject Matter Expert.
Product Road map	Starting with a product vision, a roadmap is a visual plan containing a potential series of incremental features over time. It guides a team by matching releases to business goals. Commonly completed on Agile/Scrum efforts.	Watermark Agile Business Analysis	Product Vision.

BA Term	Definition/Use	Reference (BABOK® Guide section unless noted)[1]	Synonyms/Notes
Product Scope			See Solution Scope.
Product Vision Statement	Description of the solution's goals and how the solution aligns with the organization's strategy. Commonly completed on Agile/Scrum efforts.	11.1.2.4, To Glossary	
Project	The *BABOK Guide* uses the concept of "Change" to describe what we typically call a project. *BABOK Guide* Definition: "A temporary endeavor undertaken to create a unique product, service, or result."	Glossary	See Change.
	A temporary endeavor undertaken to achieve a unique product, service, or result.	BA Practice Guide[9]	
Project Manager	*BABOK Guide* Stakeholder definition: "Project managers are responsible for managing the work required to deliver a solution that meets a business need, and for ensuring that the project's objectives are met while balancing the project factors including scope, budget, schedule, resources, quality, and risk."	2.4.7, Glossary	Project Lead.

9   Project Management Institute. *Business Analysis for Practitioners: A Practice Guide*. Newtown Square, PA: Project Management Institute, Inc., 2015. Copyright and all rights reserved. Material from this publication has been reproduced with the permission of PMI.

BA Term	Definition/Use	Reference (BABOK® Guide section unless noted)[1]	Synonyms/Notes
	The person who is responsible for achieving the project objectives.	BA Practice Guide[10]	
	The role responsible for ensuring that the end product or solution is delivered within the project's constraints of time, budget, resources, and quality. Project managers take input from stakeholders, such as the business analyst, and incorporate it into the overall project management plan.	Larson and Larson, Glossary	
Project Scope	The work needed to deliver a product, service, or result that meets the business need.	Glossary	
Proof of Concept	A low-fidelity model that is used to validate whether a proposed solution is feasible. It does not "test" the appearance of the solution, the software itself or materials used to create it, or the processes that will be followed when using the solution.	10.36.3.2, Glossary	Proof of Principle. See Prototype.
Prototype	An early model and the output from the technique Prototyping.	10.36.3.2, Glossary	See Prototyping.

10   Project Management Institute. *Business Analysis for Practitioners: A Practice Guide*. Newtown Square, PA: Project Management Institute, Inc., 2015. Copyright and all rights reserved. Material from this publication has been reproduced with the permission of PMI.

BA Term	Definition/Use	Reference (BABOK® Guide section unless noted)[1]	Synonyms/Notes
	Used to document navigation, design, usability, errors, messages, and the look and feel of the end product without investing the time and resources needed for full development. Prototypes can be low- or high-tech, making use of technology or completed with "paper and pencil."	Larson & Larson, p. 57	
Prototyping	An iterative technique to validate stakeholder needs. It provides early feedback using a visual mock-up of an interface. Can be "horizontal" for navigation or "vertical" for details (data). Prototypes can provide feedback on the user experience, as a way to evaluate design options, and as a basis for future development of the solution. Types include Throwaway ("paper-pencil") and Evolutionary (Functional). Methods include Storyboarding, Paper Prototyping, Workflow Modeling, and Simulation.	10.36	

BA Term	Definition/Use	Reference (BABOK® Guide section unless noted)[1]	Synonyms/Notes
Quality	The *BABOK Guide* definition: "The degree to which a set of inherent characteristics fulfills needs." When defining the Quality and Quality Attributes, the *BABOK Guide* uses the word "system" instead of "solution." The term "quality" is used throughout the *BABOK Guide* but is not a specific competency, technique, or task output. This is the same concept but stated differently from a more traditional definition: **ISO 8402:** "The total features and characteristics of a product or service that bears its ability to satisfy stated or implied needs."	Glossary	
Quality Assurance	The *BABOK Guide* definition: "A set of activities that are performed to ensure that a process will deliver products that meet an appropriate level of quality." The *BABOK Guide* itself does not refer to quality assurance outside the domain of testing, which is not part of the business analysis activities.	Glossary	
Quality Attributes	The *BABOK Guide* definition: "A set of measures used to judge the overall quality of a system."	10.30.2, Glossary	See Nonfunctional Requirements.

BA Term	Definition/Use	Reference (BABOK® Guide section unless noted)[1]	Synonyms/Notes
Questionnaire	A set of defined questions used to collect information.	Glossary	See Survey/Questionnaire.
RACI Matrix	A matrix for recording stakeholder roles/responsibilities. Stands for **R**esponsible, **A**ccountable, **C**onsulted, **I**nformed. The *BABOK Guide* says it's best used at the Initiative (think Project) level.	10.39, 10.39.3.2, 10.43.3, Glossary	Roles & Permissions Matrix, Responsibility Assignment Matrix. See Stakeholder List.
	A common responsibility assignment matrix to define the involvement of stakeholders related to their work on projects.	BA Practice Guide.[11]	
	Used to categorize the major areas of responsibility of a project or other work. **R**esponsible (who does the work), **A**ccountable (approves, makes the decisions, signs off), **C**onsult with (whose input is needed) and **I**nform (who do we need to inform after the work is done).	Larson and Larson, Glossary	

11 Project Management Institute. *Business Analysis for Practitioners: A Practice Guide*. Newtown Square, PA: Project Management Institute, Inc., 2015. Copyright and all rights reserved. Material from this publication has been reproduced with the permission of PMI.

BA Term	Definition/Use	Reference (BABOK® Guide section unless noted)[1]	Synonyms/Notes
Referential Integrity	Each foreign key in a database entity or table has a matching primary key in a related entity/table.	Simsion, p. 60, Watermark Data Modeling	See Foreign Key, Primary Key.
Regulator	A stakeholder who is responsible for the definition and enforcement of standards.	2.4.8, Glossary	See Role.
Relationship	Many different relationships can be found in modeling techniques. A **Data Modeling** relationship visually shows the significant business connections between two entities or classes. In a **Business Model Canvas,** a customer relationship is mentioned. In the Fishbone Diagram, it shows the connection between cause and effect.	10.8, 10.15; 10.40.3.1	Association. See Data Modeling.
Release Planning	The process of determining which requirements or user stories to include in a release, phase, or iteration, based on the value that can be delivered in an increment or "release" of software or other products.	6.4.4.5. Larson & Larson, p. 120	Planning Workshop.
Repository	A place or method for storing and retrieving things. May be used for short- or long-term storage or be a real/virtual location.	Glossary	Store, Warehouse.

BA Term	Definition/Use	Reference (BABOK® Guide section unless noted)[1]	Synonyms/Notes
Request for Information (RFI)	An elicitation method (*BABOK Guide* says it has to be formal) before beginning the procurement process. Often a fact-finding document, used early in a selection process when the requester is open to a number of possible options. It requests information from vendors about potential solutions to a given need.	10.49.2, Glossary	
Request for Proposal (RFP)	Used to request proposals to solve a specified business need typically from a small number of potential vendors. The solutions could vary and are part of the proposal. The *BABOK Guide* says it is a formal document. In sum it is a request for requirements of a potential solution. The RFP initiates the procurement process. In order to create an RFP, the enterprise's requirements have to be defined. After these requirements are sent to the vendor, the vendor matches the requirements of the solution to those of the organization and returns a bid.	10.49.2, Glossary	
	In short, a document designed to obtain bids and proposals from vendors.	Larson and Larson, Glossary	

BA Term	Definition/Use	Reference (BABOK® Guide section unless noted)[1]	Synonyms/Notes
Request for Quote (RFQ)	Used to request bids on a specific solution from a number of potential vendors. An RFQ is less formal than an RFP and may be a subset of an RFP.	10.49.2, Glossary	
Request for Tender (RFT)	One way to assess vendor reliability and capabilities. An open invitation to vendors to submit a proposal for goods or services.	10.49.2, Glossary	
Requirement	The *BABOK Guide* calls a requirement a "usable representation of a need." Other common definitions include:	2.2	
	(1) A condition or capability needed by a stakeholder to solve a problem or achieve an objective. (2) A condition or capability that must be met or possessed by a system or system component to satisfy a contract, standard, specification, or other formally imposed documents. (3) A documented representation of a condition or capability as in (1) or (2).	These are based on IEEE Standard 610, 1990	
	Describes the features, functions, capabilities, and characteristics of the end product, solution, or component of a solution. It satisfies a business need (which can also be a want or expectation) and allows stakeholders to do something or know something new or different from what they have today.	Larson & Larson, Glossary	

BA Term	Definition/Use	Reference (BABOK® Guide section unless noted)[1]	Synonyms/Notes
	A statement of customer need or objective, or of a condition or capability that a product must possess to satisfy such a need or objective. A property that a product must have to provide value to a stakeholder.	Wiegers & Beatty, Glossary	
Requirements Attribute	A characteristic, property of or fact about a requirement. Requirements attributes are used in Traceability, particularly if a traceability matrix is used. It is used to help manage requirements.	3.4.4.6, 5.2.4.2, Glossary	
Requirements Allocation	Assigning (allocating) the requirements that will be built and released with each solution component.	7.5.4.3, Glossary	
Requirements Architecture	A structure or organized arrangement for requirements, including any relationships between them. Similar to, but separate from tracing of requirements. Primarily about how the requirements are organized, which models are used, and relationships (such as dependencies) between requirements. The interrelationship of requirements comprising the solution or solution component.	7.4.2, Glossary	
Requirements Artifact	A work product developed during business analysis that contains a concrete deliverable. Examples include diagrams, elicitation results, and documentation.	Glossary	Work Product, Product Deliverable.

BA Term	Definition/Use	Reference (BABOK® Guide section unless noted)[1]	Synonyms/Notes
Requirements Baseline			See Baseline.
Requirements Classification Schema	Identifies levels or types of requirements to allow for categorization.	Section 2, 2.3	See Requirements Types.
Requirements Defect	A problem or error with a requirement. Can be found during requirements validation (it does not add value) or verification (it's not correct).	Glossary	See Defect.
Requirements Life Cycle	All requirements and designs go through different stages called a life cycle that takes them from creation to retirement.	Chapter 5, Glossary	
Requirements Management	Includes planning, executing, controlling the work of elicitation and collaboration, Requirements Analysis and Design Definition, and Requirements Life Cycle Management.	3.3, Glossary	
Requirements Management Plan	A subset of the business analysis plan that is used to describe the activities, deliverables, and roles relating to managing the requirements.	Glossary	See Business Analysis Plan.

BA Term	Definition/Use	Reference (BABOK® Guide section unless noted)[1]	Synonyms/Notes
Requirements Management Tools	Software that supports requirements management. It often includes such things as the ability to trace, model, and document requirements.	5.1.4.3, Glossary	
Requirements Model	A (usually) graphical representation or abstraction of the current or future state of the solution.	Glossary	
Requirements Package	Comprehensive set of requirements used for presentation to stakeholders. Requirements may be "packaged" at any point in a project. It facilitates a common understanding of the requirements among all stakeholders, and it documents that understanding for future reference. It may be used as a requirements baseline.	Glossary	Requirements Document.
Requirements Review			See Reviews.
Requirements Sign-off			See Approve Requirements, Governance.
Requirements Structure			See Requirements Architecture.

BA Term	Definition/Use	Reference (BABOK® Guide section unless noted)[1]	Synonyms/Notes
Requirements Traceability			See Traceability.
Requirements Types	The following classification schema is used to describe requirements: **B**usiness Requirements **S**takeholder Requirements **S**olution Requirements **F**unctional **N**onfunctional **T**ransition Requirements	2.3	See Requirements Classification Schema.
Requirements Validation	Work done to ensure requirements and designs are within scope and will address the stated need.	7.3.2, Glossary,	See Validate Requirements, Validation.
Requirements Verification	Work done to ensure requirements and designs are correct and follow approved standards.	7.2.2, Glossary	See Verify Requirements, Verification.
Return on Investment (ROI)	One way to measure value. Average ratio of money earned or lost over some time period, compared with what was invested.	10.20.3.5, Glossary	

BA Term	Definition/Use	Reference (BABOK® Guide section unless noted)[1]	Synonyms/Notes
Risk	The BABOK Guide defines a risk as "the effect of an uncertainty on the value of change, the solution, or the enterprise." Although risks can have positive or negative effects on value, the BABOK Guide emphasizes that it only deals with negative impacts.	2.2, 6.3.1, Glossary	
	An uncertain event or condition that could impact one or more project objectives positively or negatively.	BA Practice Guide	
	A future event that if it occurred, could affect various outcomes. Risks can be positive or negative.	Larson and Larson, Glossary	
	"A condition that could cause some loss or otherwise threaten the success of a project."	Wiegers and Beatty, Glossary	
Risk Analysis and Management	The process of identifying, analyzing, evaluating, and managing uncertainties in order to minimize potential negative impact on value of the change, solution, or enterprise.	10.38	

BA Term	Definition/Use	Reference (BABOK® Guide section unless noted)[1]	Synonyms/Notes
Risk Assessment	From the *BABOK Guide*: A task to "understand undesirable consequences of external and internal forces on an enterprise during a transition."	6.3, Glossary	Risk Quantification.
Risk Register	A matrix that supports analysis and assessment of identified risks and a plan for dealing with them.	10.38, Figure 10.38.1	
Risk Response Plan	Determines the best approach to deal with a given risk, once it's been assessed: Mitigate, Avoid, Transfer, Accept, and Increase are the five risk responses the *BABOK Guide* specifies. There is an apparent contradiction in the *BABOK Guide*. In the introduction to the task, it notes as "Important" that it will only discuss negative impacts on value. One response noted in 10.38.3.4 is Increase as a way to seize an opportunity.	6.3	Risk Response Strategy
Risk Tolerance	A stakeholder's or enterprise's ability to endure risks. The *BABOK Guide* describes three broad categories: Risk Aversion, Neutrality, and Risk-Seeking.	6.3.4.4	

BA Term	Definition/Use	Reference (BABOK® Guide section unless noted)[1]	Synonyms/Notes
ROI			See Return on Investment.
Role	In process modeling, the type of person, group, or even a system that participates in a process.	7.1.4.1, 10.35.3.1	Actor. See Organizational Modeling.
	The function that a team member performs, such as coding and testing.	BA Practice Guide, Glossary[12]	
Rolling Wave Estimation	The estimates are refined throughout the change (project). Detailed estimates are provided for near-future phases or iterations. Based on what is known, the remainder of the initiative is estimated by extrapolating what is known and projecting the remaining work.	10.19.3.1	See Estimate, Rough Order of Magnitude Estimation.

12   Project Management Institute. *Business Analysis for Practitioners: A Practice Guide*. Newtown Square, PA: Project Management Institute, Inc., 2015. Copyright and all rights reserved. Material from this publication has been reproduced with the permission of PMI.

BA Term	Definition/Use	Reference (BABOK® Guide section unless noted)[1]	Synonyms/Notes
	Progressive refinements of estimates as new project phases or iterations begin. Provides detail for activities that are known, with continuous refinement as more becomes known. At the beginning of a phase or iteration, the upcoming phase or iteration is estimated with more accuracy and future phases are estimated with analogous or ROM estimates (see Analogous and ROM Estimation Techniques). Example: a BA provides detailed estimates for upcoming eliciting and documenting requirements from a retail operations team, and a high level estimate for the analysis and subsequent modeling efforts for those requirements. Once requirements are elicited, the BA can provide a detailed estimate for analysis and modeling.	Larson & Larson, p. 124, Watermark Learning project management course.	
Root Cause	The heart of the problem that has no underlying problem.	10.40.2, Glossary	
Root Cause Analysis	A structured technique used to analyze problems that have been identified and uncover the source or "root" cause(s) of business problems. Several types of analytical tools can be used, and Fishbone Diagrams and Five Whys are the two mentioned in the BABOK Guide.	10.40, Glossary	Problem Analysis.

BA Term	Definition/Use	Reference (BABOK® Guide section unless noted)[1]	Synonyms/Notes
	Technique used to determine the cause of one or more variances, defects, and risks.	BA Practice Guide, Glossary[13]	
	"An activity that seeks to understand underlying factors that contribute to an observed problem."	Wiegers and Beatty, Glossary	
Rough Order of Magnitude Estimation	A high-level estimate based on limited information. A wide range of variance is applied, such as -50% to +50%. For example, a rough estimate might be to take 20 hours to develop a business process model, which could be as few as 10 hours or as many as 30.	10.19.3.1	ROM Estimate. See Estimate.
Scenario	In the *BABOK Guide* listed with Use Cases. Describes the interaction of an actor (person, system, etc.) with the solution.	10.47	See Use Cases and Scenarios.
Scope	The boundaries of the change (think project), the solution (think product), or a need.	1.4.6.1, Glossary	

13   Project Management Institute. *Business Analysis for Practitioners: A Practice Guide.* Newtown Square, PA: Project Management Institute, Inc., 2015. Copyright and all rights reserved. Material from this publication has been reproduced with the permission of PMI.

BA Term	Definition/Use	Reference (BABOK® Guide section unless noted)[1]	Synonyms/Notes
Scope Modeling	A technique used to define the boundaries (scope) of a solution. The *BABOK Guide* emphasizes that scope modeling helps put elements inside or outside of those boundaries. Elements can be any aspect of the project, which the *BABOK Guide* calls "Change."	10.41	Context Diagram, Scope Model.
Scrum	A framework of lightweight practices for developing products, and the most popular Agile method. Work is done in 1-4 week Sprints, with a goal to produce a usable product increment of sufficient quality to be potentially releasable.	11.1.3.1	See Product Backlog, Sprint.
	Scrum uses a Product Backlog to manage the desired product features and functions, with backlog items chosen for a Sprint (or iteration). At the end of the Sprint, the product increment is shown to stakeholders for feedback, which may change the content or priority of items on the Product Backlog. Retrospectives are performed at the end of every Sprint.	Watermark Agile Business Analysis	

BA Term	Definition/Use	Reference (BABOK® Guide section unless noted)[1]	Synonyms/Notes
Scrum, Daily	The Daily Scrum occurs every 24 hours during a sprint and is facilitated by the Scrum Master. The meeting is short (around 15 minutes), and often held standing up to prevent people from getting too comfortable and prolonging the meeting. The purpose of the Daily Scrum is to communicate what has occurred during the past 24 hours, what is planned and what obstacles, or impediments, are preventing the team from moving forward.	Watermark Agile Business Analysis	Daily Stand-up.
Scrum Master	The role in Scrum that guides a team, but facilitates rather than directs the tasks of planning, scheduling, and work division.	11.1.2.2	Agile Team Leader, Coach.
Secondary Actor	Part of use cases in which an actor supports the execution of the use case, but does not trigger the use case.	10.47, Glossary	
Sequence Diagram	A UML (Unified Modeling Language) diagram and *BABOK Guide* technique used to model interactions between objects in a system using the sequence of logic for different scenarios. It models the logic of scenarios by showing the information passed between objects in the system (solution) through execution of the scenario.	10.42, Glossary	See Message.
Service	Work performed for stakeholders from their perspective.	Glossary	

BA Term	Definition/Use	Reference (BABOK® Guide section unless noted)[1]	Synonyms/Notes
SIPOC	The *BABOK Guide* calls it a table or tool that describes inputs and outputs relating to multiple processes or process elements. SIPOC stands for Suppliers/Inputs/Processes/Outputs/Customers.	10.34.3.4, 10.35.3, Glossary	
SME			See Domain Subject Matter Expert and Subject Matter Expert.
Solution	A BABOK Core Concept. The *BABOK Guide* defines a solution as "A specific way of satisfying one or more needs in a context." A solution satisfies a need by resolving a problem or enabling stakeholders to take advantage of an opportunity. In practical terms it describes output of a proposed or actual change.	Table 2.1.1, Glossary	
Solution Approach, Determine	Task definition: "Describes the general approach that will be taken to create or acquire the new capabilities required to meet the business need." One activity needed to develop alternatives for the solution is to determine what approach will be taken for the solution. For example, a solution could be a proprietary, internally-developed solution or bought from a commercial vendor.	7.5	Define Design Option.

BA Term	Definition/Use	Reference (BABOK® Guide section unless noted)[1]	Synonyms/Notes
Solution Component	One aspect or part of the overall solution. Examples of a component are processes, organizational structures, new networks, different parts of a large software solution, etc.	Glossary	
Solution Evaluation	KA definition: describes the tasks needed to "assess the performance of and value delivered by a solution." A solution may not bring value for several reasons. For example, it might function as specified, but not provide any value to the enterprise. Or it might have terrible performance once volumes increase. This KA completes an assessment and recommends needed changes to the solution. This assessment can happen at any point during the change. That is, the solution does not have to be implemented before assessing its performance and value.	Chapter 8	
Solution Life Cycle	The states of a solution from inception to its retirement.	Glossary	Product Life Cycle.

BA Term	Definition/Use	Reference (BABOK® Guide section unless noted)[1]	Synonyms/Notes
Solution Requirements	Describe the characteristics of a solution that meet business requirements and stakeholder requirements. They are developed and defined through requirements analysis. They are frequently divided into subcategories, particularly when the requirements describe a software solution: **functional** and **nonfunctional**. Functional requirements describe capabilities and nonfunctional requirements describe quality of service, without which the solution will not provide value.	2.3	
Solution Scope	The "set of capabilities" (think deliverables) that must be produced to address the business need. Also includes how the solution will affect the business, its operations, and its technology.	6.4.4.1, Glossary	Product Scope.
Specify and Model Requirements	Taking the output from elicitation and creating requirements and designs. The *BABOK Guide* calls these "representations." The *BABOK Guide* also reminds us that requirements are representations of the need and designs are representations of the solution.	7.1	

BA Term	Definition/Use	Reference (BABOK® Guide section unless noted)[1]	Synonyms/Notes
Sponsor	The person responsible for providing resources for an effort (project, program, portfolio), and for enabling its success.	BA Practice Guide[14]	
	Has the role of project owner. Provides the project funding and is responsible for key business decisions.	Larson & Larson, Glossary	
Sprint	A short development cycle that delivers incremental components of business functionality. Typically lasting one month or less, each sprint is intended to produce working software or other outputs that can be delivered to a customer.	11.1.3.1	See Iteration, Scrum.
Sprint Planning	A ceremony that produces a description of the user stories to be completed in the sprint, all the tasks that are required to produce the user story, and an estimate of the effort to complete each task.	Larson & Larson, p. 120	Iteration Planning.

14   Project Management Institute. *Business Analysis for Practitioners: A Practice Guide*. Newtown Square, PA: Project Management Institute, Inc., 2015. Copyright and all rights reserved. Material from this publication has been reproduced with the permission of PMI.

BA Term	Definition/Use	Reference (BABOK® Guide section unless noted)[1]	Synonyms/Notes
Sprint Zero	The period before the first development iteration begins, in which some or all of the following occur: • The team is formed • The team's physical and development environments are set up • The vision is defined • The initial Product Backlog is created • The initial setup, delivery, and iterations are planned • The architecture is envisioned	Ambler, Scott Watermark Agile Business Analysis	Iteration 0.
Stakeholder	A BABOK Core Concept. A person or group that has a stake or interest in the success of a change (think project), the need, or the solution. Includes Business Analyst, Customer, SME, End User, Project Manager, Regulator, Sponsor, Suppliers, and Tester.	Table 2.1.1, 2.4, Glossary	
	Stakeholders might be affected or they might just perceive that they are affected by project, program, or portfolio activities, decisions, and outcomes.	BA Practice Guide[15]	

15   Project Management Institute. *Business Analysis for Practitioners: A Practice Guide*. Newtown Square, PA: Project Management Institute, Inc., 2015. Copyright and all rights reserved. Material from this publication has been reproduced with the permission of PMI.

BA Term	Definition/Use	Reference (BABOK® Guide section unless noted)[1]	Synonyms/Notes
	Stakeholders have a vested interest and can be impacted both positively and negatively by either the project or the end-result of the project. Stakeholders can be individuals or groups, as in a stakeholder group.	Larson & Larson, Glossary	
	Are affected by or can influence the process or outcome.	Wiegers & Beatty, Glossary	
Stakeholder Analysis	Identification and analysis of stakeholders or stakeholder groups who may be affected by a change (again, think initiative or project). The analysis includes assessing the impact of the solution to the stakeholders and determining where their participation is needed. Stakeholder Analysis is performed throughout the business analysis work.	3.2.4, Glossary	
Stakeholder List/Map/ Personas	Table or matrix of stakeholders affected by the change, by the solution, or by the need itself. Used to perform stakeholder analysis and to document stakeholder characteristics, such as levels of authority, stakeholder attitudes, and levels of decision-making authority.	10.43, Glossary	Influence Map. See RACI Matrix.

BA Term	Definition/Use	Reference (BABOK® Guide section unless noted)[1]	Synonyms/Notes
Stakeholder Proxy	A substitute for the Product Owner on Scrum projects. The *BABOK Guide* expands this definition, saying it's any time a business analyst represents the stakeholder's needs.	11.1.1, Glossary	
Stakeholder Requirements	*BABOK Guide* definition: "Stakeholder Requirements describe the needs of the stakeholder that must be met in order to achieve the business requirements." Stakeholder requirements describe the requirements from the perspective of the stakeholder and help ensure that the more detailed Solution Requirements align with the Business Requirements. They are developed and defined through business analysis."	2.3, Glossary	
State Modeling	A technique that diagrams various "states" that an entity/class goes through during its lifetime. Transitions move an entity from state to state based on events or other triggers.	10.44	State Diagram; See Transition, State. AKA State Machine Diagram, State Transition Diagram, Entity Life-Cycle Diagram. See Transition, State.

BA Term	Definition/Use	Reference (BABOK® Guide section unless noted)[1]	Synonyms/Notes
Stated Requirement	A requirement that has been articulated during business analysis. It occurs throughout business analysis.	Glossary	
Statement of Work (SOW)	A formal statement of the need. Different SOWs have different levels of detail. Mentioned in passing as one input to the Change Strategy	6.4.2, Glossary	
Stereotype	Additional properties of a class. In UML (Unified Modeling Language), these are so-called extensions to UML to create new elements. They are abstractions that apply to things like Use Case relationships (<<Extend>> and <<Include>>) or to Classes (e.g., <<actor>>).	10.15, Figure 10.15.2	
Storyboarding	One of the three prototyping methods, this shows the sequence of activities visually and with text showing the interactions of the end user with the solution.	10.36.3	See Prototyping.
Story Point	As one way to complete relative estimation, story point estimation is a team estimation technique representing the relative complexity to develop a user story.	11.1.3.2,	

BA Term	Definition/Use	Reference (BABOK® Guide section unless noted)[1]	Synonyms/Notes
	The relative complexity for developing a user story, based on an arbitrary scale. It represents the total effort a story would take to develop. Two common methods for estimating story points are Tee-Shirt Sizes (XS, S, M, L, XL) and Fibonacci Series (1, 2, 3, 5, 8, 13, 20, 40, 100)	Larson & Larson, p. 121	
Strategy	An approach that will be taken to meet goals and objectives.	Chapter 6, Glossary	
Strategy Analysis	The business analysis work to identify the business need, enable the organization to address that need, and integrate the strategy into the organization's strategies.	1.4.2, Section 6	See Strategy.
Subject Matter Expert (SME)	Business and technical stakeholders who have expertise in their domain. Business SMEs (domain SMEs) provide input into the product/solution requirements. Technical SMEs provide input into technical direction and constraints.	Larson & Larson, Glossary	See Domain Subject Matter Expert.
Sunk Cost	The time and effort already invested in an initiative to date. Although money spent (sunk costs) cannot be recovered, stakeholders are often reluctant to cancel failing initiatives, having a tendency to "throw good money after bad." Despite this reluctance to cancel an effort or eliminate an existing solution or solution component, sunk costs should not be considered when determining future actions.	8.5.4.2	

BA Term	Definition/Use	Reference (BABOK® Guide section unless noted)[1]	Synonyms/Notes
Subtype/ Supertype	In data modeling, an entity that has general attributes (supertype) with variations of the entity (subtypes) having unique attributes. For example, a bank's Account entity has generic facts, with a Checking Account, Savings Account, Certificate of Deposit, and Loan each having unique attributes placed in separate subtypes.	Simsion, p. 117, Watermark Data Modeling	Parent/Child. See Generalization.
Supplier	A stakeholder outside the boundary of the organization that provides products or services.	2.4.10, Glossary	Provider, Vendor, Consultant.
Survey/ Questionnaire	A technique that allows collecting a large amount of both qualitative and quantitative information from people, in a fairly short amount of time. Best used when a large number of responses to a limited set of questions are needed quickly. According to the BABOK Guide, questions can be either open- or closed-ended.	10.45, Glossary	
Swimlane	Segregated bands on a process model diagram that show which roles perform which parts of a process. Flows that cross boundaries indicate the passage of work to another role, and usually involve a "handoff" (input or output).	10.35.3.1, Glossary	See Process Modeling.

BA Term	Definition/Use	Reference (BABOK® Guide section unless noted)[1]	Synonyms/Notes
SWOT Analysis	A strategic planning technique, categorizing an organization's **S**trengths, **W**eaknesses, **O**pportunities and **T**hreats to internal and external conditions. Also useful for a framework for opportunity analysis, competitive analysis, and business and product development.	10.46, Glossary	Strategic Planning, See Competitive Analysis.
Systems Thinking	*BABOK Guide* definition: A way to think about how people, processes, and technology interact holistically. [Wikipedia definition]: Systems thinkers consider that: A "system" is a dynamic and complex whole, interacting as a structured functional unit; Information flows between the different elements that compose the system; A system is a community situated within an environment; Information flows from and to the surrounding environment via semi-permeable . . . boundaries.	9.1.5	
Task	Any activity completed during business analysis.	1.4.3, Glossary	
Technique	A method or tool to help perform business analysis tasks.	1.4.5, Glossary	

BA Term	Definition/Use	Reference (BABOK® Guide section unless noted)[1]	Synonyms/Notes
Temporal Event	In use cases, an actor that triggers a system response based on a time period, such as weekly.	10.47.3.2, Glossary	
Throwaway Prototype	A temporary prototype created with low-fidelity tools, such as paper and pencil or PowerPoint.	10.36.3.1, Glossary	See Prototyping.
Time Boxing	A requirements prioritization technique that fits work into a fixed "box" of time, such as 2 weeks or 90 days. Requirements are then prioritized based on the most important requirements that can be accomplished in the time box. Time Boxing prioritizes work by fixing the available time and number of resources and determining the amount of work (scope) that can get done in that amount of time with that number of resources.	10.33.3.3, Glossary	Budgeting, Time-Box.
Traceability	The ability to track requirement and designs through the development life cycle. It should be bi-directional; to trace requirements backward to the business need for them, and forward through implementation. Traceability also covers the relationship of requirements to each other.	5.1.2	Requirements Traceability.

BA Term	Definition/Use	Reference (BABOK® Guide section unless noted)[1]	Synonyms/Notes
	Ability to track "product requirements from their source to the deliverables that satisfy them." This definition does not provide for the ability to track requirements back to the business need.	BA Practice Guide, Glossary[16]	
	The ability to track a requirement back to the business need and forward to implementation through the development life cycle. Traceability helps ensure that each requirement 1) Adds value by tracing it to the business need, 2) Is defined completely and correctly by tracing each higher-level requirement to its components and each component to the higher-level requirement, and 3) That has been approved is implemented. Traceability helps manage scope by preventing rogue requirements from slipping unnoticed into the project.	Larson & Larson, Glossary	
	Process of defining logical links between one system element and another.	Wiegers & Beatty, Glossary	

---

16   Project Management Institute. *Business Analysis for Practitioners: A Practice Guide*. Newtown Square, PA: Project Management Institute, Inc., 2015. Copyright and all rights reserved. Material from this publication has been reproduced with the permission of PMI.

BA Term	Definition/Use	Reference (BABOK® Guide section unless noted)[1]	Synonyms/Notes
Transition, State	In State diagrams, an event or other trigger that causes an entity to move from one state to another. Business rules dictate which transitions are valid for which states.	10.44.3.2	See State Modeling.
Transition Requirements	Requirements for temporary capabilities in order to transition through a change (think project) from an existing to a new solution. Examples include data conversion, building "bridges" to new systems, and business continuity." Schema description: "Capabilities that the solution must have in order to facilitate transition from the current state to the future state, but that will not be needed once that change is complete. They are differentiated from other requirements types because they are temporary in nature." Data conversion, training, and other "roll-out" functions are examples.	2.3, Glossary	Implementation Requirements.
UML	Unified Modeling Language, as specified by the Object Management Group (OMG). It represents a set of modeling standards for analysis modeling techniques mentioned in the *BABOK Guide* including Activity, Class, Use Case, State, and Sequence Diagrams.	Glossary	

BA Term	Definition/Use	Reference (BABOK® Guide section unless noted)[1]	Synonyms/Notes
Usability	From the *BABOK Guide* "ease of which the user can learn to use the solution." ISO Definition: The extent to which a product can be used by specified users to achieve specified goals with effectiveness, efficiency, and satisfaction in a specified context of use.	10.30.3.1, 10.36.3.2	
Use Cases and Scenarios	A modeling technique that combines 1) a graphical system overview showing actors, use cases, and their interfaces, and 2) written descriptions that detail the interactions between actors and the solution in order for the actor to achieve a goal.	10.47, Glossary	See Scenario.
Use Case Diagram	A visual representation of the system and its boundaries. They display use cases in scope of the solution, and show which actors interact with the use cases within the solution. Diagrams can also show relationships between use cases and also between actors.	10.47.3.1, Glossary	See UML.
Use Case Flow of Events	Written series of steps performed by actors or by the solution (i.e., system) that enables an actor to achieve a goal.	10.47.3.2	Use Case Narrative.

BA Term	Definition/Use	Reference (BABOK® Guide section unless noted)[1]	Synonyms/Notes
Use Case Model	Describes the interaction in the form of a two-way "conversation" between an actor and a system. The system can be an automated system, a business process, a piece of equipment, or any combination. Ideally the use case descriptions focus on the interaction process steps, rather than including extraneous components such as data. Use case narrative flows describe the routine steps, as well as alternate and exception paths.	Larson & Larson, p. 56	
User Acceptance Test (UAT)	Using preestablished acceptance criteria, evaluates the solution against those criteria to find discrepancies and errors in the solution and determine if it meets the needs of stakeholders. Usually created and conducted by the end user.	Glossary	
User Stories	Descriptions that solution functionality requirements at a high, narrative level. Written in a short, concise statement by users (product owner in Agile Scrum), the focus is on stating the value of functionality to an individual stakeholder value.	10.48, Glossary	

BA Term	Definition/Use	Reference (BABOK® Guide section unless noted)[1]	Synonyms/Notes
	User stories are written in a short, textual format that is most often associated with an Agile/Scrum project. They are short narratives that document requested product features. One format is the user **role**, their **goal**, and their **motivation** written in the first person. For example, as an advertising administrator **(role)** I can attach any number of markets to a promotion **(goal)** so that I can replenish product needed for the promotions **(motivation).**	Larson & Larson, p. 132	
Validate Requirements	Ensures requirements and designs align to and support the business requirements and that they add value. In other words, to validate that stakeholder, solution, and transition requirements meet business needs. The process of validating requirements is ongoing.	7.3.3	See Requirements Validation.
Validation	Although not a task or technique, it is referred to throughout the *BABOK Guide* in relation to a process to determine that requirements and designs meet the business need and are in scope.	Glossary	See Requirements Validation.
Validated Requirement	An output from the task Validate Requirements in the Requirements Analysis and Design Definition KA, a validated requirement is on that is deemed by the authorized stakeholders likely to support delivery of the expected value	7.3.8, Glossary	See Requirements Validation.

BA Term	Definition/Use	Reference (BABOK® Guide section unless noted)[1]	Synonyms/Notes
Value	A BABOK Core Concept. Usefulness or worth of something to a stakeholder within the context of the initiative. In other words, something might have more value in one context than in another.	Table 2.1.1., Glossary	
Value Stream Mapping (VSM)	A diagram representing the sequence of activities required by the enterprise to deliver a product or service to the end customer, known as an end-to-end process. Usually includes activities that occur before initial inputs enter an organization and after the final outputs leave the enterprise.	10.34.3.4, 10.35.3.1, Glossary	
Variance, Performance	The difference between expected performance and the actual performance.	8.2.4.5	
Vendor Assessment	A technique to evaluate and assess the potential of vendors to meet their commitments when called on to provide products or services for a solution.	10.49	
Verification	Although not a task or technique, it is referred to throughout the *BABOK Guide* in relation to a process to determine correctness.	Glossary	See Requirements Verification.

BA Term	Definition/Use	Reference (BABOK® Guide section unless noted)[1]	Synonyms/Notes
Verify Requirements	Ensures requirements and designs are defined clearly enough to allow solution design and implementation to begin. Also that they meet the quality standards defined in advance. Helps ensure requirements are usable.	7.2.2	See Requirements Verification.
Verified Requirement	An output from the task Verify Requirements in the Requirements Analysis and Design Definition KA, a verified requirement is on that is deemed correct (acceptable level of detail and follows standards) by the authorized stakeholders.	7.2.8, Glossary	See Requirements Verification.
Viewpoint	Defines how requirements and designs will represented, organized, and related to each other.	7.4.4.1, Glossary	
Walk-through	A review of some kind of work product or set of work products to identify, validate, and verify requirements and designs.	10.37.3.2, Glossary	See Inspection, Peer Review.
Work Breakdown Structure (WBS)	An estimation technique that hierarchically breaks down or decomposes work into manageable pieces. A WBS can break "endeavors" (note that the *BABOK Guide* goes out of its way to avoid the use of the term "project") into phases, milestones, activities/tasks, and deliverables into smaller units.	10.19.3, 10.22.3.2, Glossary	Functional Decomposition. See Estimate.

BA Term	Definition/Use	Reference (BABOK® Guide section unless noted)[1]	Synonyms/Notes
	A hierarchical decomposition of the scope of work.	BA Practice Guide[17]	
	A technique to help plan scope. It hierarchically decomposes deliverables into smaller, more manageable components. Some software management tools also refer to the hierarchy of activities and tasks as a WBS.	Larson & Larson, Glossary	
Work Product	Used to describe any **by-product** of any initiative including documents, notes, diagrams, etc. Such by-products are used to record and organize information and help in analyzing and evaluating requirements and designs. Examples are meeting agendas, interview notes, throwaway prototypes, etc.	Glossary	

17   Project Management Institute. *Business Analysis for Practitioners: A Practice Guide*. Newtown Square, PA: Project Management Institute, Inc., 2015. Copyright and all rights reserved. Material from this publication has been reproduced with the permission of PMI.

BA Term	Definition/Use	Reference (BABOK® Guide section unless noted)[1]	Synonyms/Notes
Workshop	A technique that elicits requirements in a structured group setting. Can be used to accomplish a variety of goals including to define scope, discover, review, prioritize, and reach closure on requirements and designs. As a facilitated event or activity, it is attended by participating stakeholders in order to achieve some kind of goal. Examples are Facilitated workshop, facilitated session; JAD.	10.50, Glossary	
XML	"XML (Extensible Markup Language) is a general-purpose specification for creating custom markup languages. It is classified as an extensible language, because it allows the user to define the mark-up elements. XML's purpose is to aid information systems in sharing structured data especially via the Internet, to encode documents, and to serialize data."	Data.gov	

Bibliography

BABOK Guide	A Guide to The Business Analysis Body of Knowledge®, Copyright 2005–2015, International Institute of Business Analysis. All rights reserved.
BA Practice Guide (*Business Analysis for Practitioners: A Practice Guide*)	Project Management Institute. *Business Analysis for Practitioners: A Practice Guide*. Newtown Square, PA: Project Management Institute, Inc., 2015. Copyright and all rights reserved. Material from this publication has been reproduced with the permission of PMI.
Data.Gov	www.data.gov/glossary
Larson and Larson	Practitioner's Guide to Requirements Management, 2nd Edition, by Elizabeth Larson and Richard Larson. Copyright 2009, 2013. All rights reserved.
Simsion	Data Modeling Essentials, by Graeme C. Simsion, Copyright 2001 The Coriolis Group. All rights reserved.

Watermark Agile Business Analysis	Watermark Learning Agile Business Analysis course manual, copyright 2008–2016.
Watermark Data Modeling	Watermark Learning Data Modeling course manual, copyright 1998–2016.
Watermark Use Case	Watermark Learning Use Case Modeling course manual, copyright 2002–2016.
Websites	Agile Manifesto: http://agilemanifesto.org/
	Ambler, Scott, 2005–2014, Agile Modeling, Requirements Envisioning, An Agile Best Practice: http://agilemodeling.com/essays/initialRequirementsModeling.htm
	Ambler, Scott, Agile Modeling Driven Development (AMDD), The Key to Scaling Agile Software Development, 2005–2014: http://agilemodeling.com/essays/amdd.htm
	Rajat Bhalia, April 29, 2015,Better Sprint Planning, Scrum Alliance website: https://www.scrumalliance.org/community/articles/2015/april/better-sprint-planning
Wiegers and Beatty	Wiegers, K. & Beatty, J, Copyright Karl Wiegers and Seilevel (2013), Microsoft Press, Redmond, WA. All references are direct quotes from this book and are used with their permission.

Business Analysis Resources

We designed our Certification materials to be comprehensive resources for your preparation for IIBA Level 1–3 exams and the PMI-PBA exam. If you want additional materials to complement this Glossary, we have you well covered.

All the Tools You Need to Pass your Certification Exam

Certification Preparation Classes
Our comprehensive workshops will prepare you for the CBAP®, CCBA®, ECBA®, PMI-PBA®, or PMP® exams and help you make the most of the limited study time you have. In-person, virtual, and self-paced editions of these classes are available.

CBAP® Version 3.0 Study Guide · PMI-PBA® Certification Study Guide
Our comprehensive study guides help you readily master all Knowledge Areas/Domains for the applicable exam and focus your study time.

CBAP®, CCBA® and ECBA® Online Study Exams · PMI-PBA® Online Study Exam · PMP® Online Study Exam
This self-paced program adapts as you progress in your exam preparation. Contains unlimited use of Warm-Up exams to get started, a Drill section to concentrate on one area at a time, and a full certification exam simulator. You get detailed feedback for each question and summary results for each exam.

BABOK® Flashcards
Colorful, sturdy flashcards that cover the most important BABOK terms and techniques. Over 300 cards to help you drill and learn the central concepts for the IIBA exams, and help you finalize your exam preparation.

BABOK® Study Tables · PMI-PBA® Study Tables
Get an overview of the Knowledge Areas/Domains for the applicable exam in a comprehensive and visual package. Our colorful robust tables help you study independently or to use with study groups or training classes.

For more information, visit www.watermarklearning.com/certification/.
We also have a number of links to free resources on our site to help you in your preparation efforts . . . and on the job.

About the Authors

Elizabeth Larson, CBAP, PMP, PMI-PBA, CSM, and Richard Larson, CBAP, PMP, PMI-PBA, are Co-Principals of Watermark Learning (www.watermarklearning.com), a globally recognized Business Analysis, Project Management, Agile, and Business Process Management training company.

For over 30 years, they have used their extensive experience in both business analysis and project management to help thousands of BA, PM, Agile, and BPM practitioners develop new skills. They have helped build Watermark's training into a unique combination of industry best practices, an engaging format, and a practical approach.

Their speaking history includes keynotes and repeat presentations for national and international conferences on five continents. They have written four industry books: *CBAP Study Guide*, *PMI-PBA Study Guide*, *The Influencing Formula*, and *Practitioners' Guide to Requirements Management*. They have also co-authored chapters published in four books, as well as numerous articles that appear regularly in BA Times, Project Times, and Modern Analyst.

Both Elizabeth and Richard are contributors to all editions of the IIBA® Business Analysis Body of Knowledge (*BABOK® Guide*) as well as the PMBOK 4th and 5th editions. In addition, the Larsons were lead authors for PMI's *Business Analysis for Practitioners: A Practice Guide*.

The Larsons are proud parents of two children and grandparents of six lively grandsons. They love to travel and have visited over 35 countries around the world.